PATHWAY TO PEACE AND JOY

PATHWAY TO PEACE AND JOY

A Workbook on Prayer for Today's Busy Person

DR. WILL HINE

Pleasant Word (a division of WinePress Publishing, PO Box 428, Enumclaw, WA 98022) functions only as book publisher. As such, the ultimate design, content, editorial accuracy, and views expressed or implied in this work are those of the author.

Unless otherwise indicated, Bible quotations are taken from Good News Bible Today's English Version. Copyright 1978 by American Bible Society.

ISBN 13: 978-1-4141-0945-9
ISBN 10: 1-4141-0945-8
Library of Congress Catalog Card Number: 2007900622

TABLE OF CONTENTS

PREFACE

This brief monograph has been a labor of love. It is based on my continuing journey as a reforming workaholic and a believing Christian. I have used, as references, writings from the scriptures and two thousand years of Christian traditions. This workbook is written for people from the Christian tradition, but people from other faiths can also benefit from its teachings.

I want to thank the Rev. Verity Jones for her encouragement, Betsy Hine for her editing, Peggy Hickox for her long-suffering clerical support, the Monks of St. Meinrad, especially Fathers Lies and Moss from whom I have learned much as well as the Carmelite sisters of Terre Haute, Indiana. Finally, Sister Margaret Kern, Sister of Providence at St. Mary-of-the Woods College, has been very helpful as my spiritual director.

Some sections are short; I wanted to write a workbook that very busy people could pick up and read even if they have only a few minutes. This workbook is meant as a first step along the pathway to peace; the bibliography contains resources for going deeper into all these issues.

This workbook is meant to be written in and can be used anywhere. The Reflections/Activities section is the key element to the workbook. The reader can do these activities anywhere as needed.

William C. Hine
2006

ORIENTATION

I want to make a few important points that serve to undergird this workbook. Christian spirituality and prayer differ from other types of meditation. As Christians, our goal is to know God and to be in communion with God through Jesus Christ and the Holy Spirit. That is our Christian calling and our only end. The fruits of the Holy Spirit (peace, joy, etc.) will flow to us because of our relationship with God. The gifts of the Holy Spirit are means, not ends. The purpose of our prayer life is not just to make us "feel good" or relaxed, but to experience God and to develop a personal relationship with God.

As active and dedicated employers and employees, we like to operate in a linear world. We are task-focused and like going from A to B to C. However, our growth in work as prayer and prayer as our work operates in a circular way and on a gentle upward incline.

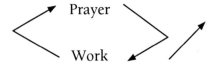

We grow, slip back, refocus, grow, slip back, and refocus *continously*. We are *never finished*. Perfection of our spirit/ prayer life is *impossible* in this life and we *should not expect it*. In fact, seeking or expecting perfection and complete peace, joy, etc. is counter-productive to our faith journey. We will experience peace, joy, insight, and growth—but always as by-products of our work and prayer. We seek only unity with God—our spiritual journey is one of purgation, enlightenment and unity with God. To use a common phrase, "no pain (in life), no gain (in our prayer life)."

We are sinners in an imperfect world seeking God through and in our work and prayer. God, Jesus Christ and the Holy Spirit are always with us but only in the present moment. Some of our main challenges as Christians are to live our faith, to practice our faith, to love God's gifts to us, and to refuse to let the dead hand of the past or worry about the future keep us from God's relationship with us TODAY. Relax and focus on God today as He is always knocking. But are we really listening?

Finally, we MUST find time in our busy, work-focused lives to practice the forms of prayer I will discuss in this workbook. Jesus prayed early in the morning and late at night. We can pray in our cars or on the train, bus, or plane while commuting or traveling. We can take a walk or close the office door at lunch to pray daily. We should *always* have a small Bible or another work of inspirational literature with us. It is not the *amount* of time, but the *quality* of time that is an important issue, along with, and most importantly, the *frequency* and *regularity* of our practice of prayer. The most precious gift we have to give to others and to God is *our time*. We need to use it wisely to keep a balance of work and prayer. The benefits are enormous, both in work and in our developing prayer life.

More than ever before, at work and in our daily life, we have to rely on ourselves to develop our careers as these days it seems that company loyalty is a thing of the past. In the future, we will have 3-6 careers in a lifetime and we will live much longer; loyalty to organizations (and vice versa) will continue to diminish; and worldwide change will continue to accelerate. What exciting and challenging times are ahead! By seeing work and prayer as two sides of the <u>same</u> coin, we can be truly blessed to be alive today to live and practice our faith.

All our prayer activity will be of little help or value if it does not lead to operative witnessing of our faith in the world as committed Christians, and here I do not mean just the traditional forms of witnessing. Our great gift is to live our faith both at work and at home so we can be examples. Do people at work respect you, and do you live your Christian principles at work? By your actions would your co-workers know you are a faith-based person? To paraphrase a popular maxim, does what you do speak so loudly they can't hear what you are saying?

Chapter 1

CHANGE AND WORK IN THE THIRD MILLENNIUM

P eople have always been faced with change, from the discovery of fire to the advent of computers. People have used their God-given imagination to push the frontiers of knowledge and information. It sounds trite but it's true: the *only* constant today is *change*. This change impacts our work life, as our work is our calling and destiny. We were meant to work in a productive way and use our work as a prayer to God. There are dozens of references in the Old and New Testaments that focus on the importance of hard work, the support of the boss for his/her staff, and the support of staff for their boss.

We always think *today* that we are challenged as never before by changes in the workplace, life styles, their resulting pressures, and so on. In my opinion, a case can be made that the rate of change faced by our great-grandparents between 1880-1920 in the Industrial Revolution, was a time of greater change than today. We moved in 40 years from our agrarian society to an industrial society. The factory model was developed and the pyramid management organizational model was born. The automobile was developed and flight was discovered. The scientific revolution, based on Newtonian physics, accelerated greatly. During this time profound changes in the K-16 education system occurred, such as the consolidations of schools, the introduction of community colleges, the development of Land Grant universities, and the development of colleges as schools to train teachers.

Today, in many ways, we are challenged with the demise of these 150-year-old paradigms and the development of new ones driven by computers, technology, the web, globalism, competition, high-energy physics, studies of the universe and clashing cultural values. Seven million new web pages are developed worldwide on a daily basis. Information on the web doubles every six months; the industrial model is changing; and great changes in medical/health care industries abound. Computers will continue to change the way we work and live in the next 25 years. Theoretical physics will change the way we look at the physical world. People will have 3-6 careers (not jobs but careers!) in a lifetime and will work more and more at home. Lifelong learning is the norm forever. In higher education, adults have moved from their roles as non-traditional students to neo-traditional students. In 10-15 years, 80% of higher education curricula will be all or in part based on and delivered using Internet technology. Experts tell us we have seven different generations alive today. It is interesting to me, as someone in my 50s, to have 30-year-olds talk about the value and attitudes of the younger generation and meaning people in their 20s! Due to these changes, we will have to *work harder* and *longer* and <u>be more responsible individuals</u> for our own work and life successes.

You might ask why a book on prayer would begin by taking a look at change and work. My thesis is simple: We need to view our work and prayer life as deeply and profoundly connected in order to live in this new millennium. We also need to be more self-directed and self-contained without losing our love for God and our fellow human beings. The church will have to focus more and more on spirituality and on those writers who discuss faith, work, and prayer together. As Christians, we must find a <u>balance</u> between our work and prayer. The Christian faith undergirds the idea that work is our calling and is therefore what God wants us to do. I believe that prayer and spirituality can help us to have a faith that works, shows us a way to lead, and supports us as moral, spiritual and ethical people. Prayer can help us as individuals to be self-reliant, become lifelong learners, work longer hours, find peace and success, be good parents, make important health-care decisions, and provide leadership in our churches. I am reminded of a cartoon showing a boss coming back from a long lunch hour. His secretary said, "You have three phone messages and there have been two new paradigm shifts since you left for lunch." All our major institutions are undergoing profound changes. How does a spiritual being who is made in the image of God and who is baptized with the Holy Spirit meet these challenges?

A writer from the middle Ages who spoke to the issue of work and prayer was Brother Lawrence. He was a simple man who wrote in a profound way. He said, "The time of business does not with me differ from the time of prayer; and in the noise and clutter of my kitchen (work), while several persons are at the same time calling for different things, I possess God in as great tranquility as if I were upon my knees at the Blessed Sacrament." When pressure of work would overtake him, he would stop and reflect on work as prayer. He believed and practiced that he was more with God at <u>work</u> than in <u>the chapel</u>, never making work only personal gain, always being humble and focusing on work as prayer.

We learn through life what to think about, and what we spend time doing shows our values and commitments. The Christian desert fathers of the third century can teach us much–through their focus on humility and quiet prayer, we can find our true selves and our callings: *Bonum est Praetolari-come cilentio salbatarae di* (It is good to wait in silence for the salvation of God.) To pray, no matter what form is taken, requires dedication and practice. God is always there, but we must clear away a place to honor God and receive His spirit. Our work, in the proper perspective, can be one of our most important prayers and gifts to our God. We must always keep inner prayer growth as a focus.

Whether you are a housewife, a husband, a teacher, a businessperson, or other professional this is what and where God wants us to be to live out our faith. God was a worker. Too often, I feel the church has tried to separate work life from church and prayer life. I strongly believe that they are *one in the same*. Our work life can and must be dedicated to God. In our work, we can have a dynamic ongoing relationship with our God. Our work should be viewed as God's activity through us. We need to see our vocation as a calling. This is important whether this vocation is being a monk, a priest, a minister, a doctor, a salesman, a businessperson, a housewife, a retired person, etc. Prayer means nothing in our life if we do not see or practice our faith in action. The idea that if one is to be successful in the secular world one cannot be a person of faith is dead wrong.

Ultimately, God is in control of all aspects of our lives, and we can gain the proper perspective and be thoroughly successful in all aspects of our work life if we remember this point. The scriptures are full of stories and examples of hard work being part of God's plan. As workers, we are co-creators with God of His plan; what a wonderful challenge! We must grow beyond being self-focused. Laziness or slothfulness is to be avoided. The pursuit of dollars is okay as long as it is not seen as an *end* but only as a *means* whereby we can share our wealth with others.

Next, we need to see our work as ministry. We need to hold onto the principle that I found in a quote attributed to Ignatius of Loyola, the founder of the Society of Jesuits. He devoted his life to very hard work, and he had much adversity in establishing this great Roman Catholic religious order. Once he was asked what he would do if the Pope ordered him to disband the Jesuits—the life work of Ignatius. He said he would go to the chapel, pray for 30 minutes, and then look for other *work* to glorify God and live out his calling. Work can deepen our relationship to God, and help us grow in self-awareness. This, to me, demonstrates the right attitude we need to have toward our work life. We must view our work as a way to live out God's plan for us and make our work an important gift to God. We must always remember that it is not the type of the work you do; but whether or not you are doing it from a faith perspective. The success of your work is not defined by the size of the paycheck.

Chapter 2

THE BENEDICTINE TRADITION OF PRAYER AND WORK

"If you would learn self-mastery begin by yielding yourself to God."

—Lobstein

The orientation of the 1500-year-old Roman Catholic Benedictine religious order to work can help to guide us today. I am reminded of a line from the movie "Rudy" when the priest is talking to Rudy and he says I only "know," for sure, two things. "There is a God and I am not Him." Prayer, no matter what the approach, is all about right relationships with God. God has given us ample direction as to what that right relationship is, especially in the area of work. We are told work is our calling; we are to work hard, productively, obediently, and honestly. Work does not have to be about pay. Being lazy, unfocused, mean spirited, and disobedient is not the right way.

Ora et Labora (Prayer & Work)

In the fifth century, St. Benedict made this concept central to how a monastery should operate. I believe this is true for all Christians today, whether in a monastery or not. The real focus on this concept, I think, is that our work is our prayer and our prayer is our work. Just as mind, body, and spirit are one, it is also true that prayer and work are two sides of the same coin. We must live our prayer life in our work and our do our work as a way to deepen our prayer life. If our prayer life is not strong, we do not have the strength, insights and peace to live our faith as humans made in the <u>image</u> <u>of</u> <u>God,</u> whether in the family, church or office. Also, our ministry (work) must exhibit our faith or we are just a "noisy gong."

I can imagine that someone reading this workbook is thinking, "is he saying work is more important to God than family? Does he mean it is okay to work 24/7 and neglect our family, church and others?" Not at all! We are our brothers' and sisters' keepers, not only at work but also in all aspects of our life!

In this millennium, we are challenged to keep an important balance between faith and work, and we will have to be careful to maintain this balance. If you see work <u>only</u> as a way to gain financial reward or status you are "doomed" to a diminished life as a Christian, and you will not be as <u>successful</u> at work as you could be. You will be subject to burnout, non-productivity and distress, and you certainly will not be living the life to which God has called you. Through prayer we can live within the proper balance of work, family and church.

Prayer, work, faith, action, effort, rest, silence, family, obedience, success, anxiety, and peace are all sides to the same coin(s)! So the ideal is to develop an active prayer life and practice it. The remainder of this book, which I hope is practical for you, contains a few brief chapters on different approaches to prayer.

The Rule of St. Benedict, which is the organizational guideline for western monasteries, applies to our work and prayer lives as Christians today in regards to our prayer and work. Below are some principles, based on the Benedictine Rule, for your prayerful thinking.

1. The most important gift we can give to God and to our fellow human beings is our time.
2. We are both human beings and human doings.
3. We must plan for daily prayer time.
4. We must practice different types of prayer, such as *Lectio Divina* (more on this later), contemplative prayer, prayers of praise and thanksgiving, intercession, and prayer walking (more later).
5. Exercise often.
6. Remember, our life is only a journey and will come to an end; the best is to follow.
7. Work is not limited to activity for remuneration. (In my life, I have received no money for some of my most important work.)
8. No matter what our age, we can all make a contribution to and be a Christian model for others.
9. The first step toward humility is obedience to God and others.

10. If someone is listening to us, we need to try, as much as is humanly possible, to remember that they are listening to Christ.
11. Pray the Psalms–pray and/or read all the Psalms at least once a year.
12. All work can be noble.
13. Work, pray and participate in communal activities with other Christians.
14. See a visitor to our church as Christ coming to our church.
15. God wants you to work.
16. Many times at our work silence is golden…
17. Mind, body and spirit are all one.

Amen.

A basic concept of the Benedictine Order is that we need to look at our vocations as our *callings*. While we have traditionally reserved "being called by God" as the purview of clergy only, this is not true. In my opinion, one of the reasons the Benedictine rule has lasted 1500 years is that it contains God's insights and they are applicable to the monk and non-monk alike. The Latin root of vocation, *vocare*, means "to call." If we are to be successful and productive in our work, we must look at our occupation in this way. God will be there to guide us and give us opportunity to witness.

Prayer helps build the relationship between us and the living God who dwells within us by virtue of our baptism. God's grace actualizes this supernatural union and helps us develop our "True Self." The benefits of prayer are enormous. Prayer strengthens us, as well as our right convictions and actions, and sustains our resolution to work and confront suffering. Prayer is the light that directs and enlightens us. For our part, prayer demands energy, perseverance, and a humble spirit. Prayer is the key to our spiritual growth. Our prayer and intentions will always be a complex mystery because they are actions and gifts from God. If we could ever completely understand the power of prayer, we would completely understand God, and then God would not be God.

We must always monitor the driving force behind work. If the driving force is only ambition or the desire of having money, which we will enjoy only briefly, it can only be an obsession. These bases for work only lead to struggle and dissatisfaction, and, in my opinion, they are short and ineffective routes into the work environment. We must see our work as prayer. The principle Christian faith must always be the North Star on our compass.

In reading Genesis, I am always struck by the images of God and Adam as <u>workers</u>. That the glory of work is part of God's plan for us seems very clear to me. In many ways, we can be at our best when we are working and working hard, but when the false, self-serving self comes to work, it can and does turn us against God's plan. Consequently, abuse of others and ourselves can happen. When we take this approach, we are not following God's plan for our life and we will not achieve what God wants us to achieve. Consequently, the fruits of the Holy Spirit will not be ours and our work could crush us. To paraphrase Thomas Merton in his outstanding book, *The New Man*, "our work ought to be a dialogue with reality (truth) and therefore conversation with God." In other words, our work must be our life prayer. God is always with us, in us, and available to us. We must keep our balance and perspective as we develop what Thomas Merton would call our "True Self." I believe prayer is central to achieving this balance. The goal, then, is to live our life and our work according to God's plan, the way God wants us to work.

Finally, as anyone in the world of work knows, bad things can happen to good people. If your career does not allow you to do your work as a calling, move on; you may not be able to do this immediately, so do what you can do and begin equipping yourself for job change.

To end this section, I want to reference the writing of Johannes Tauler, a great fourteenth century Christian mystic. In his writing he emphasized that, for the laity, our work is the major way we live and grow in our faith. Mary Brian Durkin says, in an article on Tauler in the 2003 summer issue of *Spiritual Life,*

> Tauler places an unusual emphasis on the role of work as a way of achieving sanctity, an idea his lay urban audience, particularly those of the rising merchant class, found appealing. There is scarcely a sermon that does not in some way refer to the importance of work. In sermon 40, he questions: Since our Heavenly Father is pure activity, is it surprising, then that we, fashioned in God's Image, should resemble Him in His activity? Why is toil or labor, both physical and mental, constantly decried as a burden? On the contrary, Tauler urges, we should look upon our work as the usual, normal way for most

of us to achieve sanctity. How can we be sanctified by our work? Tauler offers succinct advice: Whether you are starting a new task or a new way of life, begin by determining that the work aims to accomplish God's will and His glory, not yours. After examining the purity of your intentions, consider the talents, virtues, and strength this work requires, then, humbly acknowledging your own insufficiency, ask the Giver of all Gifts for guidance and the requisite graces, humility, love, and prudence, needed for satisfactory completion of the work.

Chapter 3

CONTEMPLATIVE PRAYER

A
n ancient form of prayer that dates back almost 2000 years to the desert fathers and mothers of the early Christian church is the quiet prayer of contemplation. Experts believe there are differences in approaches; I want to present a brief overview. Only in the last 50 years with the writings of Thomas Merton, Charles Keating, Henri Nouwen, and Basil Pennington, just to name a few, have Christians begun to practice this deepest and, some might say, purest form of prayer. We are spiritual beings on a life journey and within each of us is the Holy Spirit/God/Christ. God is always "knocking" but we must quiet ourselves in order to "taste and see" the fruits and guidance of God's grace. The God within can be a healing prayer for us but we must make time for the Holy Spirit to heal us and give us the fruits of the Holy Spirit.

Contemplative prayer may not be for everyone, and we may experience times of "dryness/desert," but stay with it.

God's healing power is always at work even if we do not know it. Taking time to listen and contemplate is good and is what we are called to do as people of faith. Finally, pray as you can, not how you are told or think you should. In any of the prayer forms we will discuss there are no "pat" formulas and no "shoulds," We are all different and unique, loved by God and made in the image of God.

Our Christian tradition is rich in resources and I will share some references at the end of the workbook on this type of prayer. To begin to do Contemplative Prayer, find a quiet, safe place where you can be alone. Secure a comfortable chair, close your eyes and take 10-15 deep slow breaths. Next, speak your mantra (word) and repeat it very slowly. If any thought or outside noise gets your attention, very gently and slowly return to saying your word and move back to praying. Do this for up to 15-20 minutes. At the end, very slowly and gently recite the Lord's Prayer and gradually begin to engage the outside world again. If the fruits of the Holy Spirit come to you, fine, but that is a *by-product,* not the *goal.* Contemplative prayer can be the greatest of all healing prayers but it takes time for our Western action-focused lives to practice this form of prayer. It will be challenging, but we can achieve great results and deepen our faith to make us better Christians and workers. Give it a try!

A closing idea about your mantra: select a word or very short statement that is meaningful to you. Some examples are Abba, Jesus, Christ, God, Jesus Prayer, Amen, Peace but choose your own.

I want to close with a list of ideas related to contemplative prayer.

1. Powerful
2. Healing
3. Quiet
4. Slowly
5. Gently
6. Practice
7. Read about
8. Grow
9. God's love
10. Focus
11. Relax
12. God's gift
13. Learn more
14. Desert/arid
15. God is always knocking
16. Soul/Holy Spirit
17. Change
18. Peace
19. Relationship
20. Unity
21. God within

Before you start practicing and after you begin doing this type of prayer, periodically return to this list to re-read it and to add words of your own.

M. Basil Pennington, a prolific and powerful writer on this type of prayer, can be an excellent resource for you if you want to read more. However, remember this: pray as you can. There are no "shoulds." If you find someone who tells you they are an expert in this type of prayer, run–don't walk–to the door! All the great writers on this type of prayer, including Teresa of Avila, St. John of the Cross, and Julian of Norwich, as well as Merton, Keating, and Pennington were all <u>very</u> <u>humble</u> <u>people</u>.

Practicing this type of prayer two times a day for up to 20 minutes is good. Some even pray longer. I myself like to do some brief scripture reading or some other type of prayer and then go into contemplative prayer. This type of prayer is a gift from God. At our Christian baptism, we are infused with one of God's greatest gifts to us, the Holy Spirit, or, as Paul Tillich called it, "the spark of infinite," our "True Self." Unfortunately most of us spend time building our external or false self. Our God is a merciful, loving God who delights in being with us and healing our egotistic self. Our job is to bring to the table the greatest gift we can give God, or, for that matter, anyone– the gift of time. We need to set aside time to be quiet and listen for God to speak and lead us.

Contemplative or centered prayer cannot be taught. Contemplative prayer is not a feeling; nor is it a *goal* of feeling *good* or less anxious. These emotions, or "fruits of the spirit," may come to us as baptized Christians and give us insights into our True Self and true reality so we can lead better more productive lives. Finally, we will go through "desert" times in our prayer life, and this may be especially true in the practice of contemplative prayer—but we must PERSIST! We do not know how God is working in our lives when we pray, and we may think that nothing is happening.

However, over time we will benefit from this type of prayer; we will change and begin to see others, the environment, the world and ourselves in a different way. Thomas Merton says, "Hell can be described as a perpetual negation from our *true being*, our true self which is in God."

Here is a list of what Contemplative Prayer is not:

- It is not a technique.
- It is not a relaxation exercise.
- It is not a form of self-hypnosis.
- It is not a charismatic gift.
- It is not a para-psychological phenomenon.
- It is not limited to the "felt" presence of God.
- It does not lead to speaking in tongues.

What Contemplative Prayer is:

- It is at the same time a relationship with God and a discipline to foster that true relationship with God.
- It is an exercise of faith, hope, and love.
- It is a movement beyond conversation with Christ to communion.
- It habituates us to the language of God which is silence.
- It puts us in touch with our True Self.
- It is a process.
- It is the simplest and purest form of prayer.

Chapter 4

LECTIO DIVINA

The Holy Scriptures are the *Word of God* for us. There are no greater outside resources Christians can draw upon to deepen our faith and work than the Holy Scriptures. A central point in our prayer life is to read/listen to the scriptures. Through praying the Holy Scriptures, we can and will have a dynamic encounter with God. We can gain wisdom and discernment and develop better relationships with God and others. Divine Reading (*Lectio Divina*) will change us and can be an important prayer response to God.

First and foremost, the attitude we must bring to our Divine Reading is humility, and second is a sense of celebration. God so loves us that he sent Jesus Christ to us and gave us the New Testament. How do we pray the scriptures to deepen our spiritual life and to guide us at home and work? We can draw upon thousands of years of Judeo-Christian tradition for our answer. The Holy Spirit will guide us as we use the scriptures to deepen our faith. *Lectio Divina* brings to the soul the message of God's love which seeks me out (St. Bernard) and we can establish a heart to heart contact with God. The Holy Scriptures are much more than messages and insights from God; they are living, dynamic encounters between God and us. In the Holy Scriptures there is the real presence of God, as all scripture is inspired by God and speaks the word of God. Just reading the scriptures <u>literally</u> is not enough! We need to hear the "breath of God" in the Holy Scriptures, which goes beyond the literal meaning. Using Bible commentaries, reading books on scriptures and so on can be very helpful and give us insights. But *Lectio Divina* is much more—this prayer is a means to a much higher and more substantial encounter with Christ/God/Holy Spirit. Starting with the eighth chapter in Nehemiah, we begin to see the prayer tradition of *Lectio Divina*. We understand the Holy Scriptures only by the grace of God; hence we must read, meditate and *pray* the Holy Scriptures. Guigo the Carthusian developed the following order for contemplative prayer.

Lectio Divina (Divine Reading)

Lectio	*Mediatio*	*Oratio*	*Contemplatio*
(Reading)	(Thinking)		(Resting)
Reading the Word	Focusing on the Word	Prayer of Thanksgiving	Resting with the Word

Selecting which Holy Scriptures to read is completely an individual decision. Some select favorite passages. Some start by reading through a book in the Bible; the four Gospels, Psalms, Ecclesiastes and Romans are favorites of some people. Start reading where you want; the only advice I can give for reading is *less is*, i.e., read short passages rather than trying to read too much at one time. Following is one approach to *Lectio Divina* for your information.

Put yourself in a quiet place, relax and take 10 deep breaths. In prayer, ask God to fill you with the Holy Spirit and open your heart to receive the Word. Some people then say three times, slowly, "Lord Jesus, send me your Spirit, renew me today."

Lectio: Reading The Word

The First Reading
- Read the selected Bible passage from beginning to end.
- After you've read the passage, spend a few moments considering the text.
- Identify its literary style: is it prose, a poem, a narrative, a monologue, a dialogue, etc.?
- Answer who, what, where, when and how.
- Can you place the passage in context? What comes before? What follows?

The Second Reading

- Re-read the passage aloud slowly.
- Picture yourself as both the story-teller or narrator and the audience.
- Read it with meaning and care.

The Third Reading

- Read the passage a final time.
- As you read, allow yourself to stop and rest with the words, phrases or images that appeal to you or call your attention.
- Consider why that word, phrase or image appeals to you or calls to you.

Meditatio–Focusing on The Word

Meditation is this phase of *Lectio Divina* wherein we converse with THE WORD. In this, we take the phrase, word, or image that spoke loudest to us and share it with God.

- Reflect on a particular phrase, word, or image.
- Ask about its importance.
- Why this word, this phrase, or this image?
- What does it say to me?
- How does it speak to my life, my relationships?
- What kind of response does it call forth from me?
- How is it inviting me to practice my faith? My discipleship?
- Say all there is to say about this word, phrase or image. Speak until all words are spoken.

Oratio–Prayer of Thanksgiving

- Having read and meditated on God's Word, we pray now in thanksgiving for our encounter with God, who inspired the Word, Jesus, who is the WORD and the Holy Spirit, who opens us to receive the Word.

- Pray a spontaneous prayer of thanksgiving.

Contemplatio–Resting with the Word

- Now that we have spoken it, is time to rest with the Word and listen. In this stage, we silence ourselves and listen for the voice of God.
- Simply sit in silence.
- Feel the quiet and let it embrace you.

The above outline is based upon some of the ideas that Father Brenden Moss spoke of during a retreat at St. Meinrad's Monastery in St. Meinrad, Indiana. *Lectio Divina* has been an important part of Christianity since the beginning of our faith. The scriptures, God's words, are central to our Christian faith. The Bible provides valuable lessons and insights into how we are to live our life. The key challenge for us in the use of this form of prayer is *listening*, because we are all much more focused on talking, leading, organizing and doing. Therein lies the challenge for us. One of the vocational work benefits of this type of prayer is that it can strengthen us to be more like *servant leaders*. The scriptures speak to us most profoundly only when we develop the discipline of listening. In this way, we can develop an intimacy with God, a oneness with God. It is only through God's grace that one can gain from the experience of *Lectio Divina*. We approach praying the scriptures as a way not only to inform us, but also to transform us. God is always present in us and in the scriptures if we will take the time and effort to listen for Him.

Chapter 5

HUMILITY AND
SOLITUDE

"As we humble our hearts the Lord will raise it to heaven."

—RB 7:8

The quote you see above is from the Rule of St. Benedict, written over 1500 years ago. It has been the basic rule or guideline for the Christian monastic movement in the West since its inception. In many ways, a monastery is like a church or any other organization that is a group of people trying to live out their faith in the world. In the monastery, one of the central virtues of the Rule is humility. Without humility, the members of the organization can have problems. St. Benedict developed 12 levels as the guidelines of humility in order for the monastery to prosper and in the same manner those steps can be applied in any organization.

In today's world, humility has gotten a "bad rap" and is sometimes associated with someone who is a weak, "milktoast" type person; a person who lets people "walk over him or her," a person who has no opinions of his or her own. However, this is not the case. The word humility actually comes from the same root word as *humus*, meaning earth and therefore means that the person is well grounded and focused in what they believe.

Based upon the Scriptures and on the Rule of St. Benedict, here is a list of the characteristics of a humble person, someone who has true Christian humility.

A humble person

Is a good listener;

Sees all as a child of God;

Is accepting (this does not necessarily mean agreement);

Is tolerant, whether coming from a "liberal" or a "conservative" viewpoint;

Believes that getting mad is unproductive;

Believes that the whole monastery (church or organization) is more important than the individual;

Is not proud, arrogant, or self serving;

Is forgiving and forgetting of the disagreements that are inevitable in organization;

Is constructive and does not gossip;

Is patient;

Is obedient to God's commandment to love one another;

Believes that as Christians we are called to live in community; and
[Add your own]

I believe that any Christian organization should strive for the goal of humility and grow in its witness to the secular world beyond its doors. These concepts are 1500 years old and are reflected in many current organizational theory practices.

Why a section on solitude in a book on prayer and work? I believe that building times of solitude into ones life is <u>absolutely</u> <u>central</u> to being <u>productive</u> at work and also to gain greater insight to ones <u>prayer</u> life. By solitude I am emphasizing the points of detachment and separation. Both detachment and separation are necessary to develop and maintain a proper perspective at work and certainly in our prayer life. The time of solitude can be very simple, meaning shutting the door at work, going for a walk, taking a break in the morning, going outdoors, and looking for a quiet place to pray. Some people even combine solitude with physical exercising. A major challenge in our busy lives is to find a place of solitude. One must find a place where one can be alone and not be disturbed. I read that one young career mother would use the bathroom as her place of solitude; she would go in, close the door, pray and read. It can be done!

There are many different ways of looking at the dynamics of solitude and I think we can gain much from the writings of Thomas Merton, the leading spiritual writer of the last 100 years, on this. Merton was a Cistercian Monk

at the Abbey of Gethsemani in Kentucky. I can highly recommend to you *any* book that he has written related to the
issues of prayer and contemplation, but especially *New Seeds
of Contemplation*. I highly recommend that you read and
reread this book. Read a page or two and then try to write
an outline. Merton's great writing contribution is based in
part upon the fact that, during his life, he lived outside the
monastery as long as he lived inside the monastery. This
equipped him to be able to speak in a powerful way to a
very wide audience, both lay and religious. He believed
that solitude gives us perspective, gives us compassion,
gives us unity with others and nature, gives us maturity
and gives us renewal and rest, which will bring calmness
and love. We will always be imperfect. We are after all on
a life journey and we will never achieve pure joy and peace
in this life. However, through solitude, we can move in that
direction.

Where and when is your place and time of solitude?

Chapter 6

OTHER FORMS
OF PRAYER

In this section, I want to discuss different types of prayers that can be beneficial to us. When we pray, we practice faith in a most meaningful and practical way. Prayer can lead us to expressions of our most profound concerns and thoughts in regards to our personal lives, and it can strengthen us in our work.

1. Prayer of Petition
    Because God already knows our needs and wants, we pray to help ourselves focus on our requests of God. He knows our pain and our concerns, but these types of prayer can give expression and focus. This personal type of prayer can bring us peace and direction so, as in all forms of prayer, take time to pray and be silent. Also, we must always remember in *all* our prayers, no matter what form, that we are seeking *God's* will, *not our* will. God always answers our

prayers, but sometimes we do not like the answer or the timing. Almighty God, your will not mine but I ask you for...

2. Prayer of Gratitude

   This form of prayer is one that is not practiced as much today as it should be. As it says in Ephesians 5:20, "Always give thanks for all things in the name of our Lord Jesus Christ." Giving thanks to God gives glory to God and puts our relationship with Him in a proper perspective. Also, prayers of thanksgiving bring into focus the many great gifts we have received from God, whether they be spiritual, environmental, material, familial, or related to our friends, work, or health. Although we have not earned these gifts, they have been given to us. Practice the prayer of thanksgiving often, as it will bring balance to our lives and help us focus on the gifts that God provides. Almighty God, thank you for...

3. Prayer of Adoration/Praise

   The book of Psalms is composed of many ways to praise God. Praise of God is an important part of our life as Christians. Acknowledging the majesty, compassion, and awesome power of God is critical to our faith journey and the understanding of our proper relationship to God. Looking at the night sky (A good hobby is astronomy because it brings the profound majesty of God's control and design to our attention.) will put our lives in proper perspective. Finally, prayers of praise bring to focus God's saving grace and action through our Lord Jesus Christ. Creator God, All is yours and...

4. Prayer and Exercise

The unity of mind, body and spirit is referred to often in the New Testament. We are holistic beings; modern science has reinforced this point. Our physical activity can benefit our sense of well-being and increase our desire for growth in other areas of our lives. Our body is truly a temple, a scaffold for our growth in mind, spirit and work. Before I go on, I am *not* talking about the obsession we have with looking younger or thinner, or the saying that one cannot be "too rich or too thin." An inordinate focus on the physical can lead to obsessive activity and hinder our important holistic development. Moderate exercise and maintaining moderate weight is the goal. I include deep breathing activities as exercises that can and will strengthen our spiritual stamina.

Design an exercise program that works for you. This will help your prayer life. If you need outside consultation(s), gyms, clubs, etc., that is fine. As in all aspects of our spirituality, the absolute key is discipline and regularity. This regular practice will reinforce the discipline and focus we need to be successful in our work and in our prayer life, which, as I have often said, is *one*.

I want to close this section with an outline of an activity that I think blends excercise and prayer. It is prayer walking, a centuries-old Christian practice. Walking, pacing and meditating can be reinforcement to help us focus and thereby deepening our spiritual work and life and gaining insights and the fruits of the Holy Spirit. Monasteries often contained walking paths or complicated labyrinths for monks to use to meditate and gain a deeper understanding of their faith. Below are some points of reference, but make sure to design an approach that *works for you*. We are all different.

1. Practice prayer walking regularly (1-3 times a week).
2. Before starting, sit quietly for a few minutes and breathe deeply.
3. Dress comfortably and *always* walk alone
4. Walk at a comfortable and easy pace. (This is *not* power walking)
5. Really look around and focus as you slowly and deeply smell the air, etc.
6. Select a phrase (e.g. Lord's Prayer) and repeat at the start of the walk.
7. Let God lead you in your prayers and thoughts. God knows what you need.
8. Finally, listen and look at nature around you. I like to think birds' "talking" is God "talking."

An excellent small book by Linus Mundy, *Prayer Walking* is a simple guide to body and soul-fitness. To paraphrase a central idea from this book, what our prayer-walk can teach us is it's all holy ground we walk on–whether that ground is in the office, in the hospital, or outdoors.

Chapter 7

REFLECTIONS/ ACTIVITIES

This section of Reflections in the workbook serves three purposes. Each reflection

- Is a way to bring focus to our prayer, work and vocational life;
- Can be read and reread to look at our prayer, work and vocational life differently; and
- Is practical and brief so that it can be read anywhere.

I would recommend you read one a day, quickly the first time through. Then reread them a second time and ponder them. Finally, read them a third time and rewrite them from your perspective. If you go through these reflections, you will find peace and joy. Always use a pencil, as when you reread and rewrite these reflections as your answers and perspectives will change.

Reflection A–Our Limits, not God's

As work-focused individuals, we are often in leadership roles, which is good to a degree. One hardly ever provides leadership or direction if they don't want to. However, we limit ourselves by not realizing that God can do much more and is *always*, ultimately, in control. We *gain* control and focus in our work and life when we conscientiously *give up* control to God. St. Teresa of Avila, a leader of the Carmelite Order, has given us some insights that we can apply to our work and, most importantly, to our prayer life. She wrote over 400 years ago; below are a few in my own words.

1. One true gift we hold dearly as Christians is eternal life (keep your eye on the prize and our ultimate gift of salvation).
2. True spirituality as a goal in all aspects of our lives requires a change in our priorities.
3. Do *not* underestimate God's generosity and goodness–*Humility* is the key.
4. Do not limit God's potential action in our work and non-work life by the limits of our own imagination.
5. The Lord is never content. He is always knocking at our door (Acts 3:1-6) as he wants a deep relationship with us.
6. Examine your spiritual desires–are they too limited?
7. Be open and listen.
8. One must take time for silence in our prayer.

9. Our job is to create space and time for God to work in us.
10. Know God is alive in us.
11. Know, accept, honor and be thankful for God's control.
12. God's Holy Spirit will always heal, calm, change and energize us.
13. Christianity at its core is a personal and mystical relationship with God through Christ.

Activity

Of these statements, which five speak to you most? Why?

_____

_____

_____

_____

_____

_____

_____

_____

_____

_____

_____

Reflection B–Spiritual Exercises

Ignatius of Loyola founded the Society of Jesus, or Jesuits religious order in the sixteenth century. The Jesuits are his great legacy. The spiritual exercises are planned/structured activities that all Christians can benefit from to deepen their faith. As Christians we can learn many things from our church leaders who, first of all, were in the same secular world as you and I. Loyola was a successful soldier who was seriously injured in battle and went through a very difficult recovery. In a deep depression, he began to read the scriptures, analyze his life, pray, and read other books; out of the recovery process, he developed his spiritual exercises from which we all can benefit.

In this reflection, I want to focus on one small idea that Loyola believed was central to developing our faith and becoming better Christians–that of "surrender" to God. Begin your thoughts on this issue by saying this prayer three times: "Gracious God, I ask for the grace that I may be able to turn my will and life over to your care."

By surrendering to God and accepting that He is in control, we can live in the present time, not in the past or in the future. *God is only in the present.* Our faith, over and over again, whether from the scriptures or the church fathers and mothers of the past, tells us that God will guide us, and we can trust that completely. Next, take a few minutes and write down your answer to these questions: "Which path(s) of my life am I unwilling to surrender to God's will and providence?" "In what ways would my life improve, and could I find peace if I surrender to God's will and put God as central in my life?"

Next, read this statement three times: "God's promise, through the teaching of Jesus Christ and the gift of the spirit, is that nothing can separate us from God's strength, support, and peace." After Loyola surrendered his life to God and through many other prayer exercises, he went on to establish the Society of Jesus. We can learn much from his life.

Activity

Rewrite the statement above in your own words.

_____

_____

_____

_____

Reflection C–The Concept of Work in the Rule of St. Benedict

The Rule of St. Benedict was written 1500 years ago but contains ideas, concepts and perspectives that are as current as today. New technologies come and go but the human condition, in many ways, stays the same. I strongly believe this is true because at our core we are spiritual beings on a human journey. Below are a few perspectives from the Rule related to the world of work today.

1. As I mentioned in the past we must balance work and prayer. We must pray and work (not only for money) to live our lives as God wants. We must be in the world but not of it.
2. Look at work as ministry.
3. Humility is a key to success in work and prayer.
4. Refrain from laziness.
5. Control anger and never hold a grudge.
6. Develop to your full potential and continue to learn and grow at work.
7. One owes obedience to bosses (a tough point sometimes).
8. Bosses must live their faith in the workplace.
9. Bosses should not be "puffed up with pride."
10. Bosses should practice servant leadership.
11. Whether a boss or a worker (we are all bosses or workers in some part of our lives), we must see each other.
12. Work in an intelligent manner and be productive.
13. Silence and listening at work are virtues.

14. Idleness is the enemy of the soul–work hard but always keep one's life in balance.
15. Sometimes we have to do what they (bosses) say but not what they do.
16. Love God, walk humbly, and love and honor your-self and fellow workers–that is the key to giving us peace.

Activity

Select three perspectives you need to work on the most.

1. _____

2. _____

3. _____

Reflection D–Work Communication

The Rule of St. Benedict has much to say about communication between leader and staff. These lessons can speak to us today in our work lives. We all play the role of leader (boss) or staff (worker) in many aspects of our lives. These relationships are important to our being successful and we must let faith speak through our actions. Below are some points for us all to think about.

1. The leader has the authority to lead but also bears the responsibility.
2. The leader should expect obedience from workers.
3. Workers can expect compassion, consolation and support from leaders.
4. A leader seeks consolation and advice widely from young and seasoned workers alike.
5. The leader can use argument, appeal and reproof but must do as much as possible in private and must focus only on the circumstance, not the individual.
6. The leader must make a strong effort to know his/her workers.
7. Aggressive control by leaders through intimidation is *never* acceptable.
8. Quick attention to and action on issues (problems) is best.
9. A leader must earn loyalty; a leader cannot demand it.
10. The leader needs to adapt his administrative approach to his/her workers and build upon those workers' strengths and interests as much as possible.

11. The leader must see his/her workers as more than just that—workers.
12. Whether a leader or worker, all opinions need to be expressed with humility.
13. The leader does everything with counsel.

Activity

The challenge is to achieve these ends in the workplace, at home, and in church. Copy the following statement and keep it with you always.

First of all, love the Lord God with your whole heart, your whole soul and all your strength, and love your neighbor as yourself. The direction is clear. Love God. Love yourself (God loves you). Love your neighbor.

Amen.

Reflection E–Being with God Always

One of the great challenges of living our Christian life today is to be present to God always. Ignatius of Loyola has some relevant current insights, even though he wrote almost 500 years ago. Ignatius saw God's presence in *all* of creation and activity. We are human/spiritual beings in the God-created physical world. We can experience God's presence by observing nature and by really looking at God's creations, both of which can be *forms of prayer* for us. Take some time to do the following exercises.

Activity

1. Very slowly walk around a park or your yard and deeply focus on and look at God's creation.
2. Make a list of ten gifts God has given you. Thank God for these gifts and do this for three days in a row.
3. Think about God's unconditional love for us–write down two ways you can practice unconditional love with a family member, friend, at home or at work. Practice this love for a week.
4. When you are driving, at every stop sign or light think in prayer how you can live your faith today and/or thank God for one of his many gifts (Also, please keep your eyes on the road!). If you don't drive–four times a day do the same exercise somewhere. Do this for one week and try to develop this reflective habit.
5. Read the 8th Psalm two times daily for one week.

1. _____

2. _____

3. _____

4. _____

5. _____

6. _____

7. _____

8. _____

9. _____

10. _____

Reflection F–Obedience I

Obedience is a difficult concept in our culture. Raised on *rugged individualism* and "do-your-own-thing" philosophies, we find obedience difficult. **While sometimes we must stand up to authority for good reasons,** the Christian faith *requires a major focus on obedience.* In many ways, a lack of obedience is the original sin!

From the rule of St. Benedict, we can learn how to look at obedience in the workplaces of today. Monasteries are *organizations* that have existed successfully in an environment of obedience for at least 1500 years in the West; hence, there are some concepts we can use. Below are some points to think about that I would like to share with you.

1. Even if one obeys, one does not have to agree, but one must never harbor ill will.
2. Ill will only hurts the one having it and keeps one from experiencing God's love and reconciliation to the fullest.
3. In conversation, especially with someone with whom you are having difficulty, ALWAYS seek first to *understand,* not to be *understood.*
4. We can learn obedience to God by obeying and serving others.
5. Obedience, care, and understanding are very similar.
6. Obeying God and trusting God's will for our lives is central to our faith and brings us the fruits of the Holy Spirit.

7. We must always try to show respect and understanding.
8. A key way that one can show obedience is to work hard and to be an asset to one's boss, company and family.
9. As bosses, if we don't show concern for and support to subordinates, we are not living our faith.
10. As bosses and leaders, no matter what the environment (e.g., work, family, church), we are accountable to our Christian principles.
11. One of the best expressions of love is obedience, even when situations are difficult.
12. Silence can lead to obedience.
13. Pray for the Spirit of obedience–God will answer.

Activity

Write a short paragraph detailing your definition of obedience.

_____

_____

_____

_____

_____

_____

_____

Reflection G–Obedience II

The reason for the second reflection on obedience (a.k.a. humility) is that this is a difficult concept for the twenty-first century Christian. Based upon my 30+ years of work experience, I am totally convinced that the successful Christian practices these virtues. We need no better role model than Jesus Christ, the suffering "servant," as to how God desires us to live. To paraphrase Thomas Merton, "God is in the pots and pans."

Activity

What are the ways you can practice these virtues at work and home?? List four ways and try living them out.

1. _____

2. _____

3. _____

4. _____

Reflection H–Experience of God by Faith

St. John of the Cross was a leader of the Carmelite religious order. He was a victim of the Spanish Inquisition, but is considered today one of the great writers on spirituality and the Christian faith. Listed below are some concepts I have seen in his writings.

1. Faith, hope and love are God's basic commitments to us.
2. God lives for and with us in the present–not in the past or future.
3. Our faith from the Holy Spirit aligns us with God and God's gifts.
4. Faith brings light and peace.
5. Faith delivers truth, not proof.
6. Faith contains the light of God for us.
7. Faith alone gives us an experience of God.
8. Believing, hoping and loving others and ourselves are our total response to God.
9. A past without God's forgiveness can be a dark night.
10. Our future without God's promise can be worrisome and can make us anxious.
11. Hope is God's gift to us in the *present* and can give us peace and perspective.
12. We must let go of the past and not worry about the future.
13. God's steadfast *promise* is that in the *present* he is in our soul and giving us the fruits of the Holy Spirit.
14. Love heals history.

15. Our security comes from God. It is God's promise to us through our faith.
16. Our hope is the risen Christ.
17. Trials can be ways to God through faith.
18. Believe, pray, hope, love and you *will* experience God.

Activity

Pray/rewrite these in your own words.

_____

_____

_____

_____

_____

_____

_____

_____

_____

_____

_____

_____

_____

Reflection I–Friendship Exercise

"How good it is, how pleasant it is for God's people to live in unity. It is like the precious oil running down Aaron's head and beard, down to the collar of his robes. It is like the dew on Mt. Hermon falling on the hill of Zion. For there God has promised his blessing, life that never ends."

–Psalms 133

Psalm 133 was one of the favorite Psalms of Ignatious of Loyola. Loyola was a high-energy person with a definite goal in mind for his new order. He always tried to interpret positively the actions of his fellow Christians and to welcome them with affection. From the very beginning, he built recreation into the life of the Jesuit Order. Time to talk, pray, laugh, and study together was very important recreation. He stressed that Jesuits must support each other and reflect God's love to one another. Let us briefly think how we might apply this idea using one of Loyola's spiritual exercises or models and apply this to work or with other communities of which you are a member.

Activity

1. What do you do to nourish love and foster compassion to your church community?

    _____

    _____

2. Pray for each member of your community(s) and ask for grace to continue building each personal relationship based on God's love for *you*.

3. Next: Bring to mind two people, one a close friend and one a person, possibly at work, with whom you are having trouble relating. Then pray, meditate and think about these questions:

1. Am I sensitive to the emotions of _(name)_?
2. In love, how can I deal with my differences with _(name)_?
3. What does my relationship with _(name)_ ffer me?
4. What do I offer _(name)_?

Reflection J–What's Going on Here?

Probably one of the greatest challenges to understanding our life experience is *when wrong things happen to good people* and *good things happen to the wrong people at work.* There is probably no conundrum that has created more controversy within the church and outside the church. It is a major reason why people leave the church and why people come to the church. As we move through our lives, we see situations where good people (as defined by standard Christian norms) experience physical suffering, emotional suffering, loss of job, loss of career, family problems, etc. It is also true that we see people who do not follow Christian principles, are not involved with the church, who intimidate others and operate in dishonorable ways prospering by today's societal standards. The old adage that we have heard many times in our lives, "it is better to be lucky than good" often *seems* to be true. So as Christians, how do we deal with these types of situations as we look at them both personally and from our Christian faith perspective? I believe there are several perspectives on this issue that we need to keep in focus and to practice. In other words, what is our role as Christians in dealing with both sides of this coin, with people who seem to be succeeding in non-Christian ways and Christian people who seem to be having great difficulty? Below is a list of some points for us all to think about:

1. As Christians, we are called to, and have the important responsibility of, giving support to good people when they are confronted with negative

situations. There is no question that we are our *brother's and sister's keeper* and that when people are going through difficult times we have a responsibility to be of support and help to them, whether it is giving wise counsel, listening or providing other types of positive support and reinforcement. This is a calling that we all have.

2. The difficult practice is that we must not feel negative about the individual who seems to be prospering through non-Christian ways; we should not seek revenge against that person, either directly or indirectly; and we should not act in a passive or aggressive manner toward that individual. Here again, we do not endorse the act, but we must see the image of God in all fellow human beings. If there is one principle that is crystal clear in our Christian faith, it is that vengeance and retribution are God's job, not ours. These negative emotions hurt and discourage us, not the other person.

3. Whether we are directly or indirectly involved, this is a time where our faith can be of great strength to us. Nowhere in the scriptures does it say that as Christians we are going to have an easy time in this life. One can even make the case that to live our Christian faith in today's world will *almost guarantee* that, in terms of society's norms, we will not always be viewed successful and might be seen as peculiar. Finally, God will always be there to support us.

Activity

Reread parts 1-3 and put them in your own words.

_____

_____

_____

_____

_____

_____

_____

_____

_____

_____

_____

_____

_____

_____

_____

_____

_____

Reflection K–More Insights from Ignatius of Loyola about our Work Life

1. What our faith also teaches us is that Christian principles will *always* see us through any difficult situation; *we are never separated from God. God is always there knocking,* if we are listening, to support us, to help us to put things in proper perspective, to reframe our attitudes, and to help us to move on and receive the fruits of the Holy Spirit.

2. Living and practicing our faith and believing Jesus Christ is our Lord and Savior guarantees us salvation and an eternity with our God and Jesus Christ. This great gift *far* surpasses anything positive or negative that could happen in our work lives. We must look at true success in the long term of our whole life, and that lifetime is just a small part of God's gift to us. This perspective can help us keep our *balance* at work and home throughout our lives.

3. People are watching us as Christians to see how we deal with or handle tough work and life situations. There is probably no better opportunity to witness for our Christian faith, both individually and corporately, than how we handle or confront life situations.

4. See our jobs as a means, not an end. Work hard; practice our faith at work and in life; and God loves me, God is always there.

5. In the movie "Rudy," a priest tells Rudy that there are only two things he knows for sure in life: "1) There is a God, and 2) I'm not Him." Who knows how in

God's plan these types of issues and situations will "spin out"? Our faith tells us there always *is a plan*. As Christians, we are to pray and live out our life plan as best we understand. People are called to different situations at different times and different circumstances, but we must consistently be living our Christian faith. In other words, let God be God. Let go–let God. Almost all my *growth* experiences in life and in faith have been or come from some negative life situation. While unpleasant, they have allowed me to look back and see that truth–then I have been able to appreciate even more the gifts and positive things and people that God has put in my life.

Activity

List five positive points about your workplace. Build upon them to increase success at work.

1. _____

2. _____

3. _____

4. _____

5. _____

Reflection L–Lectio Divina–Praying the Scripture

This Latin phrase, *Lectio Divina*, has many interpretations and perspectives but at its center it means, "reading the scriptures." As Christians today we are blessed with the word of God in the Old and New Testament. *Lectio Divina* can be an important part of our prayer life but we have to bring certain attitudes, predispositions and, most importantly, *time* to receive the *full power* of God's love and direction that is in the scriptures. For us, the Holy Scriptures are one of God's great gifts to us.

Activity

So how should we practice *Lectio Divina* today? Reread the chapter on *Lectio Divina* and then write out an outline of this prayer practice in your own words. Select three different scripture passages and follow this prayer form.

1. _____

_____

2. _____

_____

3. _____

_____

_____

Reflection M–Symptoms of Inner Peace at Work

After you practice some of these prayer suggestions, be on the lookout for symptoms of inner peace. The hearts of a great many have *already* been exposed to inner peace using these prayer approaches, and it is possible that people everywhere could come down with these symptoms in epidemic proportions. This could pose a serious threat to what has been, up to now, a fairly stable long-term condition of conflict in the world.

Some signs to look for might include

- A tendency to think and act spontaneously rather than based on past experiences;
- An unmistakable ability to enjoy each moment;
- A loss of interest in judging other people;
- A loss of interest in interpreting the actions of others;
- A loss of interest in conflict;
- A loss of the ability to worry a lot; (This is a very serious symptom.)
- Frequent, overwhelming episodes of appreciation for God;
- Contented feelings of connectedness with others and nature;
- Frequent attacks of smiling;
- An increasing tendency to let things happen rather than make them happen; and
- An increased susceptibility to the love offered by others as well as the uncontrollable urge to extend love to others.

Activity

Pick four statements and practice them for three weeks, then pick four more and practice.

1. _____

2. _____

3. _____

4. _____

Reflection N–Ignatius of Loyola, The Examination of Conscience

Take a few minutes to do this little exercise.

An examination of consciousness is one practice that Ignatius of Loyola suggests for Christian discernment. It is also useful for the beginning of journal writing or preparing for spiritual direction. You may make your own examination by using the following suggestions of Ignatius.

Say, "God, my Creator, I am totally dependent on you. Everything is a gift from you. All is a gift. I give you thanks and praise for the gifts of this day. Holy Spirit, I believe you work in and through time to reveal *me* to myself. Please give me an increased awareness of how you are guiding and shaping my work life, as well as a more sensitive awareness of the obstacles I put in your way."

You have been present in my life today. Be near, now, as I reflect on these things:

- Your presence in the events of today;
- Your presence in the feelings I experienced today;
- Your call to me; and
- My response to you

Activity–pray the following:

God, I ask your loving forgiveness and healing. The particular event of this day I most want healed is

_____.

Filled with hope and firm belief in your love and power, I entrust myself to your care and strongly affirm _____(claim the gift at work that you most desire, most need: *believe* that God desires to give you that gift if it is good for you).

Reflection O–Anxious at Work?

Anxiety and the work place go hand in hand. This anxiety will be counterproductive and make us less focused and out of sync with living and doing God's plan in our vocation. I am absolutely certain that God sometimes uses anxiety to bring us closer to him. Here I am not talking about severe anxiety that can come to all of us during those times that we might need some outside support and help.

As Douglas John Hall writes in his book *God and Human Suffering,* "there are forms of suffering which *belong* in God's intention, to the human condition." Hall argues that anxiety is one of those important forms of suffering. Without anxiety, Hall says, we human beings would not and could not be *all* that God intends for us to be."

Next time an anxious situation presents itself at work (which many times involves other people), pray briefly and do the following five minute exercise.

1. Step away from the situation.
2. Breathe deeply/slowly 10-15 times and focus on God.
3. Pray to God to show you how this anxious moment can be used in your living out God's will
4. Go forth

Activity

Practice this process.

Reflection P–Troubles at Work *or* Opportunities for Service (to God)

For much of my 30 years experience in administration and teaching, my job has been to be in control. For the first 20+ of those years I believed completely (I was a slow learner) that I <u>was</u> in control. I saw every issue as a problem to control, manage and handle. After a really tough time in my life, I began to see the illusion under which I was operating. I learned that I was not in control and that issues or situations at work or in life should be viewed as an opportunity for service and a way to live out and practice my faith. This is a puzzle to be solved using God's strength and insights. By finding ways to live my faith in the work place, I became more effective and much more focused and calm. Think about it in your work place situation. Make a list of work issues that make you anxious. Give up trying to control them—always let go to let God be in control.

Activity

List Your Issues   List your Response

_____   _____

_____   _____

_____   _____

_____   _____

_____   _____

_____   _____

Reflection Q–Nothing New under the Sun

Those of us who are administrators, bosses, and leaders think that we need to be abreast of the newest administrative theory or practice. We think that the latest administrative theory we follow is something that is *new* and *unique*. It is humbling and good to learn that 1500 years ago St. Benedict, who established the Monastic Movement in the West, developed a list of attributes that the monastery, and all those in it should practice to be successful. The work-focused administrators today can learn much that will make us more successful in our personal lives, in our work lives and, most importantly, in our lifelong faith journeys. Below are some thoughts and words. Reflect on them and use them in all aspects of your life. I truly believe that all these concepts are well-grounded in our Christian faith, traditions, and scripture.

1. Practice humility.
2. View humility as an attribute in subordinates, staff and bosses.
3. Live your faith.
4. Support and recognize productive behavior.
5. Always address unproductive behavior with employees in private.
6. Avoid favoritism.
7. Use private discussion and counsel and reproof when necessary.
8. Accept the role of accountability and responsibility.
9. Do not keep a "black book" (e.g. to get even).

10. Your staff *will* model your behavior.
11. See how your staff and colleagues relate to subordinates, *not bosses* (This gives a truer picture related to their long-term productivity).
12. Work hard *and* smart.
13. Get rest and maintain balance in *work–prayer–recreation*.
14. Do not hire prideful staff.
15. Hire mature, temperate staff.
16. Avoid staff that is offensive, overly excitable or very aggressive.
17. Loyalty is *earned*, never demanded.
18. Remember that a kind word is a great gift.
19. Pray often in private for the fruits of the Spirit and guidance are life's challenges.
20. Live and lead in the present, not the past or the future.
21. Never hire overly controlling or obsessive staff.
22. Plan for the future but be flexible.
23. Some of our most productive time is in being with, observing and listening to God and others, *not in action* or in always doing the talking.

Activity

Read daily for two weeks.

Reflection R–Using our Talents

The old adage that money is the root of all evil is wrong. It is the love of money that leads to trouble, anxiety and non productivity. In Matthew 25:14-30, we find the parable of the talents. The central point in this parable is that hard work, the maximum use of our God-given talents, is to be desired. The hard working servants are rewarded.

Another place in the Bible that speaks to the virtue of hard work is Proverbs, the book of great practical insights and common sense. In at least 11 different scripture references, the virtue of hard, dedicated work is emphasized.

See Proverbs
6:6-11
10:4, 26
12:24, 27
13:4
15:19
19:15, 24
20:4
21:25
22:13
24:30-34
26:13-16

Activity

Put these scriptures in your words.

_____

_____

Reflection S–Death

"To the good man to die is gain. The foolish fear death as the greatest of evils, the wise desire it as a rest after labors and the end of ill."

—St. Ambrose

Think about death daily. Now, before you skip this page and turn to the next reflection, please read on. I am <u>not</u> talking about a morbid or obsessive dwelling on the subject. Pope Paul said we live today in a culture of death. He was right. Worldwide, this is especially true for Christians today. Some experts believe more Christians worldwide are suffering and dying today in many different ways for their FAITH than at any time in Christian history. What we are focusing on is a health attitude and perspective in regards to our life.

Activity

I would suggest we all ponder the following.

1. Pray daily for fellow Christians who suffer/die for their faith.
2. Think very briefly about one's sure death. (It helps keep one's "eye" on the real prize/goal of our faith and keeps a long-term perspective.)
3. Let the thought of one's death lead to living a greater and more productive life!
4. Let the thought of one's death lead to living a more balanced life at work.

Reflection T–Successes in the Office

Many times we hit home runs at work. We work-focused people are highly valued at work. We come early and leave late; however, we must not overdo it. If we take too much personal pride in our successful work activities–watch out! *Any* success we have at work is a gift from God, as all of life is a blessing from or is blessed by God. If we examine *any* successful work, we can see God's hand in it with the support of other people, good timing and maybe even a little God given luck. This very liberating idea keeps work issues in proper perspectives. Conversely, sometimes failures are not our fault, either. Our calling as Christians is to be "instruments of God" in our work and lives.

Activity

List three times you have been successful at work and look for God's hand in them. Thank God for them. Do this activity once a week for two months.

1. _____

2. _____

3. _____

Reflection U–Scheduling/Analyzing

This reflection is a challenging one that will take time and *will always* be a work in progress in our lives. Think about the following and list your responses. Revisit them after three months and see how you are doing.

Activity

1. Write a job description for your life. (e.g. goals, values, qualifications, responsibilities)
2. Write a response to the following.

Your Christian baptism lays on you the difficult task to be a Christian disciple where you are–in your workplaces, in social encounters, and, of course, in the home. If we accept that God has put each of us in a certain place—be it a factory, a boardroom, at home, in college, or wherever—then that is the place where we are called to exercise a royal priesthood as Christians in the world. What is God calling you to be and do? How can your work life be a statement of your Christian faith?

Reflection V–Who are we?

"I praise you because you are to be feared; all you do is strange and wonderful."

—Psalms 139:14

I was doing some *Lectio Divina* reading one day and prayed this verse–the more I thought about it, the more it brought into focus that all we are comes from God. All in life is either blessed or a blessing, either God wills it or allows it. Who knows how God uses our personality, both our strengths and our weaknesses in order to help us develop our faith and His kingdom. Why would God do that? Why would God take that approach? To say that one knows the mind of God is the height of conceit. We do know God is in total control and uses all of the experiences we have to help our faith and trust in God. Another name for God might be Surprise. We all carry psychological baggage, worries, and problems–that is the human condition. In order to grow in our faith and in our trust in God, we need to look at these negative situations as times for growth in our faith, as a time to refocus on God, to pray, to seek his guidance, peace and direction. Look for God's presence in our life and work. Ask God for quieter minds to listen to our heart and to the Holy Spirit that is in us.

Activity

Reflect back on the last six months at work and list four times God's presence was there. He was, is and always will be there.

1. _____

2. _____

3. _____

4. _____

Reflection W–Peace and Joy

Because God wants us to be productive, we were made to work and to try to make important contributions to our job. Peace, joy and contentment often elude us. We cannot find them, so we try to compensate by working harder and faster and isolating ourselves more and more from God and others. One of the reasons we can't find them by working harder and faster is that the answer is not outside of us, in society, in friends, or in things, or even in the church. The answer always lies within. At first that can be very difficult for us to understand, especially those of us who are hard workers, because we always seek that outside validation. So what shall we do?

Activity

Make a list of the times that you are stressed and anxious at work; when you have worries and upsets and are not focused. See if there are any common issues, ideas, misplaced values, or emphases on what other people think. Always remember that God is the *only* evaluator that counts.

List

_____

_____

_____

_____

_____

Reflection X–It's Just not Fair!

It's just not right! In our lives with God, all of us have many issues, situations and people who cross our paths. These events present us with opportunities, some good and some bad, some negative and some positive. Tribulation is a part of all our lives. Christians are not immune to tribulation; it rains equally on the just and the unjust. Thomas Merton, in his book *Dialogue on Silence*, discusses what tribulation can do in our journey to help us toward a deeper faith.

1) Tribulations can detach us from things, our ideals, or from our false self, which emphasizes again we are human beings not human doings.

2) Tribulation can help us to withdraw from vain pursuits and to focus on important issues in our life (e.g., deepening our Christian faith) to which, as Christians, we have no higher calling on our time or efforts. Tribulation helps us to appreciate the times and people in our lives.

3) Tribulation guides us as Christians to rely on the Lord and belong only to God.

4) Tribulation hurts, but it can lead to growth in our Christian faith. It's just not *fair* that we as Christians always have to suffer tribulation! Or is it?

Activity

Some tribulation has given you some insight into your Christian faith and helped you grow. How did prayer help?

_____

_____

_____

_____

_____

_____

_____

_____

Reflection Y–Salvation

This reflection on salvation is important to a workbook on work and vocation because I believe it speaks to a core issue in helping us be successful and centered. Salvation expresses the idea of the great unearned gift of God through Christ to our eternal life. Our salvation guarantees to all baptized and practicing Christians the unearned spiritual healing and eternal blessing given by our loving compassionate God. Every other activity is secondary to this point. There is no more important activity in our life than this.

Activity

Reread this statement and write your own version. Put a copy beside your bed and reread often.

_____

_____

_____

_____

_____

_____

_____

_____

_____

Reflection Z

Review the previous reflections and pick one that was most meaningful to you.

Activity

Rewrite it.

_____

_____

_____

_____

_____

_____

_____

_____

_____

_____

_____

_____

_____

Chapter 8

FOOD FOR THOUGHT

P oems are ways to communicate profound ideas in
simple ways. People can read the same poem and
see different things. God speaks to us in many ways
and poems are one way to hear His voice. I have included
this section of poems to be used when one has a brief moment during the workday for reflection. Some of them have
blank lines for you to add your own words. At the end of
the chapter are some blank pages for your own poem. I
would strongly encourage you to write your own, as it is
a wonderful way to know and see God in different ways.
One's faith can be <u>enhanced</u> by writing a poem, revising
one's poem and can be a marker of one's spiritual journey
and growth. Anyone can write poems and I believe it helps
the writer (and hopefully the reader) to "see" what is <u>true</u>
<u>and</u> <u>important</u>.

This chapter is devoted to the practice of poetry and
prayer. There is no doubt that the reading and writing of

poetry can bring focus, depth and growth to one's prayer life. Many outstanding poets, Blake and Livingstone to name a few, through their poems can help us to follow and to benefit from their spiritual pilgrimage. I would recommend to you the book, *Poetry as Prayer: The Hound of Heaven*, as a good introduction to the concept of poems and prayer. The poem, "The Hound of Heaven," is profound and moving and is a prayer to which we can all relate.

GLASS OF WATER

Half empty?
Half full?
New perspective
Water is the gift
Think about the water.

SLOW DOWN

I am told to slow down
I don't
I am told to smell the flowers
I don't
I am told to relax
I don't
I need to listen to others more
I don't
What's the problem?
Could it be the I?

THE COMMUTE

Eighteen years
same road
same scenery
same time
same views
same ole, same ole
is
all I see
But
today is different
I "SEE."
The farmer in his field
and
the field in the farmer
a
oneness
rooted in each other
The road
straight
winding
guiding me
taking me
to my destination
The bean fields
like a green ocean
rolling/waving as far as the eye can see.
The clouds in the far distance
looking like a mountain range, snow capped
moving

standing still
The corn,
tall
straight
leaves looking like hands outstretched up to God.
God in nature
Nature in God
God in me
me in God
me in nature
One.
I really "SEE" today.
Amen.

Now

Time always on my mind.
Past issues, events, hurts
Hold us
Future worries, issues,
Challenges hold us,
Tired, unfocused
Thinking about past/future
Stop
Now is the <u>only</u> <u>reality</u>,
Now is <u>all</u> we really have
Now is <u>all</u> there is.

Now–II

Now is God,
God is Now,
God with us.
Us with God.
I see God,
God sees me.
Peace
All is given
Given is all.
Amen.

Fairness

Life's not fair.
God's not fair.
I know what's fair.
Do I?

Blessing

Life is a Blessing,
When life goes well,
When we feel good
When family is whole,
When work is fulfilling,
Feeling blessed,
Easy

BUT

Life is not always a Blessing,
We fear, anxious, angry,
Family in turmoil,
Job is difficult,
Health is poor.
It rains on just/unjust,
All is God given,
All is blessings.
Find the blessings!

BLESSINGS

See opportunity in my difficult situation
Grow in faith (trust).
Help others.
Pray with fellow Christians.
Be obedient to God/Scriptures.
Talk to God.
See, really See Nature–All created world is from God.
God's peace passes all human thinking.
Amen.

SURPRISE

God is powerful.
God is all knowing.
God is creator.
Yes,

But God is most of all
Surprise/Love
Gift
Love

_____ ?
_____ ?
_____ ?
_____ ?

Amen.

SIDES OF A COIN

Being alone–
Being with
I loose myself
I find myself.
God is everywhere.
God is no where.
To truly love is to lose,
To lose is to truly love
Beginning leads to end
End leads to new beginning.
Christ in us,
Us in Christ.
Holy Spirit in Us,
Us in Holy Spirit.
To live is to die to oneself,
To die to oneself is to live.

THANKFULNESS

Thankfulness
Leads to blessings
Blessings lead to thankfulness.
Blessings are always surprise
God is surprise.

SUMMER DANCE

Birds flying
Birds landing
Birds singing
Birds eating
Trees standing
Flowers blooming
God speaking
God dancing.
I am part of this Dance,
Me in the Dance,
Dance in Me.

EYE

Nature looks at me,
I look at nature.
God looks at me,
I look at God,
God meets me.
Thank God

For eye
or is it I?
Amen.

BEING

To Be
Or
To Do?
To Do
or
To Be?
To Be
is ok.

TRYING

I try to live as God wants
I pray, attend church
I try to live according to faith
I seek happiness
But I fail
My prayer life falters
Dry
I am anxious
I am angry
I gain little from church
Where is God
How do I serve God
Is it in the trying?
Amen.

JOY

God is love
God is creator
God is now
Past, no God
Future, no God
God provides
Joy
Peace
Rest
Happiness–events can change
Joy is always in the now,
Joy God's gift.
Amen.

MORNING

Ugh or Ahh!
My eyes open
Another day
Am I grateful
or
Sorrowful?
Do I see opportunity?
or
Do I see problems?
Is the new day
A guest
or

An intruder?
Am I Excited
or
Sad
God is with us
God is within us
God is pure Love
Ugh or ahh?

CANVAS

Our life is a white canvas
Others paint on it
Events paint on it
The most important
Gift is the
Canvas–not
What is painted on it.

TREE & ME

Me and tree,
Tree and me
I need the tree
Tree needs me
Amen.

QUIET

Quiet brings peace
Quiet brings calm
Quiet brings noise
Quiet brings distraction
Quiet is void
Quiet is now
Quiet is forever
Quiet seems forever
Quiet seems an instant
Quiet brings sadness
Quiet brings happiness

Quiet _____

Quiet _____

Why?

RELATIONSHIP

Spring comes
Sun rises
Trees bloom
Flowers blossom
Grass turns green
I live.
Thanks be to God.

STILL

Be still,
Listen
Hear nothing
Ahh!

FAITH

What is Faith?
Beliefs?
Church?
Traditions?
Rituals?
No
Trust
All is Trust

A TREE

God's gift
Doing God's will
Branch is like
Hands lifted
Up to God.
Roots deeply
Anchored
A haven for
God's creatures
Living/breathing

Supporting
Changes/grows/matures
We can learn much from a tree!

Odd Couples

Loss or gain
Gain or loss
True self or false self
False self or true self
To gain is to lose
To lose is to gain
Difficult–yes
Impossible–no

Jesus Christ & Me

I seek Jesus Christ
I seek peace
I need Jesus Christ
Where is Jesus Christ to be found?
In office–yes
In nature–yes
In supernatural/spiritual–yes
In the Catholic Churches–yes
In other people–yes
In me–yes
Jesus Christ found me!
Thanks be to Jesus Christ.

WORLD'S VIEW

Fame
Wealth
Position/stuff
Face saving
Control

_____

_____

_____

?

GOD'S VIEW

Service
Humanity
Faith/trust
Cheerfulness
Compassion
Being

_____ ?
_____ ?
_____ ?
_____ ?

Which approach
Will bring
Peace
Contentment?

WHAT'S REAL?

Busy days
Meetings
Events
Speeches
Uptight, anxious
Why?
I look out the backdoor window
See nothing
Gray, dead
But I stop and
Sit–look again.
Count 20 birds in the trees
Birds on the fence
All in winter colors
Trees gently moving
Birds flying
A oneness
A connection
Which is real?
Which is from God?

GOD–HOW?

I feel this needs to pray
But how?
For what?
How do I discern
That I am praying

What God wants?
I and you
Perhaps I need to focus on the God within–silence
God within
God without
Mirrors of each other
God's way
Peace.

Workbook pages (use pencil)

_____

_____

_____

_____

_____

_____

_____

_____

_____

_____

_____

_____

_____

_____

_____

_____

_____

_____

_____

_____

SUMMARY

I am a reforming workaholic! As my father worked until he was well into his 80s and as working hard is a predisposition in our family, I am naturally inclined toward work. I have been blessed with success in my professional field of higher education. Those of us who are workaholics are highly valued today. We come in early, leave late, and are well suited to be very successful in this new millenium. But while our success at work is good, we must *also* live and practice the Christian faith in our day-to-day life. How do we balance our work life as practicing Christians? As I have written, we can stand on a 4000-year-old Judeo-Christian tradition that can be a rock and guide for us in the new millenium.

The key, I believe, is a growing and vibrant prayer and spiritual life. I do not pretend that I am an <u>expert</u> <u>on</u> <u>prayer</u> or that this short workbook contains any great new insights. If there is anything original in this workbook, it is in putting together a variety of ideas, concepts, and practices into one short monograph. I have provided some references for you to peruse. This monograph was to be a simple overview, a beginning discussion of these issues written from the humble perspective of a fellow Christian on the same journey as the reader. I have drawn upon ideas and concepts from thousands, even hundreds of years ago as well as some written in the 90s. With the <u>change</u> today, we are being as challenged as those in the first century A.D., the Dark Ages, the impact of the printing press, scientific revolution, industrial revolution and now the technology/computer revolution. However, in many ways the human condition is similar through all the ages. The reason we can learn from the past is that at our core we are <u>not</u> human beings on a <u>spiritual</u> journey through life but <u>spiritual</u> <u>beings</u> on a <u>human</u> journey through life. That is why Christian writers from long ago can and do speak to us today. This book was written from a Christian faith tradition, but contains ideas that translate to other faith traditions. Relax, stay focused, work hard, and live your faith. The absolute eternal best is yet to come.

Bibliography/ Resources

I can recommend all these books to you as ways to deepen your prayer life.

Bergan, Jacqueline Syrup & Schwan, Marie. *Praying with Ignatius of Loyola.*
Winond: Saint Mary's Press, 1991

Byre, Lavinia. *The Life and Wisdom of Benedict.*
New York: Alba House, 1998

Chervin, Ronda De Sola. *Quotable Saints.*
Ann Arbor: Servant Publications, 1992

Chittister, Joan. *The Rule of Benedict.*
New York: Crossroad, 1995

Colledge, Edmund & Walsh, James. *The Life of the Soul.*
New York: Paulist, 1996

De Waal, Esther. *Living with Contradiction.*
Harrisburgh: Morehouse, 1989

Duportal, Marguerite. *Carrying Your Troubles Well.*
Manchester: Sophia Institute Press, 1998

Durkin, Mary Brian. "Johannes Tauler, OP: Preacher and Teacher for Today" *Spiritual Life* Summer 2003: p. 100

Foxe, John. *Foxe's Christian Martyrs of the World.* Uhrichsville: Barbour & Co., 1989

Guenther, Margaret. *Holy Listening.* Bostone: Cowley Press, 1992

Kelsey, Morton T. *The Other Side of Silence.* New York: Paulist Press, 1976

Lawrence, Bruce B. *The Complete Idiot's Guide to Religions Online.* Indianapolis: Alpha Books

McGreal, Wilfrid. *John of the Cross.* Liguori: Press, 1997

Merton, Thomas. *New Man.* New York: Farrar-Straus Cudahy, 1961

Merton, Thomas. *Spiritual Direction and Meditation.* Liturgical Press, 1960

Merton, Thomas. *Thomas Merton: New Seeds of Contemplation.* New York: New Directions Publishing Company, 1961

Merton, Thomas. *Thoughts in Solitude.* Boston: Shambhala Press, 1993

Merton, Thomas. *What is Contemplation?* Springfield: Templegate Press, 1978

Mueller, Joan. *Faithful Listening.* Kansas City: Sheed & Ward Press, 1996

Munday, Linus. *A Retreat with Desert Mystics.* Cincinnati: St. Anthony Messenger Press, 1989

Nouwen, Henri J. M. *A Cry for Mercy.*
New York: Orbis Press, 1981

Nouwen, Henri J.M. *Henri Nouwen.*
Springfield: Templegate Press, 1988

Nouwen, Henri J. M. *With Open Hands.*
New York: Ballantine, 1972

Padavano, Anthony, J. *A Retreat with Thomas Merton.*
Cincinnati: St. Anthony Messenger Press, 1995

Parry, Abbot, OSB. *The Rule of Saint Benedict.*
Graceiving: Herefordshire, 1990

Paulsell, William O. *Taste and See.*
St. Louis: Chalice Press, 1992

Pennington, M. Basil *Centered Living.*
New York: Doubleday Press, 1986

Pennington, M. Basil. *Centered Prayer.*
New York: Doubleday, 1980

Pennington, M. Basil. *Daily We Touch Him.*
New York: Doubleday, 1977

Pennington, M. Basil. *Lectio Divina.*
New York: Crossroad Publishing, 1998

Rahner, Hugo. *Ignatius the Theologian.*
San Francisco: Ignatius Press, 1964

Reininger, Gustave. *The Diversity of Centering Prayer.*
New York: Continuum Press, 1999

Sebring, Ron. *Inner Peace.*
St. Louis: CBP, 1990

Sibley, Brian. *The Wisdom of C.S. Lewis.*
Louisville: Westminister John Knox Press, 1997

St. Romain, Phillip. *The Logic of Happiness.*
Liguori: Triumph Press, 1994

Vest, Norvene. *Friend of the Soul.*
Boston: Cowley Publications, 1997

Walsh, James and Tugwell, Simon. *The Cloud of Unknowing.*
New Jersey: Paulist Press, 1981

Ward, Benedicta & Anthony, Metropolitan. *The Sayings of the Desert Fathers.*
Kalamazoo: Cistercian, 1975

Weber, Alison. *Teresa of Avila.*
Princeton: Princeton University Press, 1960

Pleasant Word

To order additional copies of this title:
Please visit our web site at
www.pleasantwordbooks.com

If you enjoyed this quality custom published book,
drop by our web site for more books and information.

www.winepressgroup.com
"Your partner in custom publishing."

Printed in the United States
119614LV00001B/151-153/A